WORKING ANIMALS

Military

WORKING ANIMALS

Military

Robert Grayson

Marshall Cavendish
Benchmark
New York

This edition first published by Marshall Cavendish Benchmark in 2011
Copyright © 2011 Amber Books Ltd

Published by Marshall Cavendish Benchmark
An imprint of Marshall Cavendish Corporation

Website: www.marshallcavendish.us

This publication represents the opinions and views of the author based on Robert Grayson's personal experience, knowledge, and research. The information in this book serves as a general guide only. The author and publisher have used their best efforts in preparing this book and disclaim liability rising directly and indirectly from the use and application of this book.

Other Marshall Cavendish Offices:
Marshall Cavendish International (Asia) Private Limited, 1 New Industrial Road, Singapore 536196 • Marshall Cavendish International (Thailand) Co Ltd. 253 Asoke, 12th Flr, Sukhumvit 21 Road, Klongtoey Nua, Wattana, Bangkok 10110, Thailand • Marshall Cavendish (Malaysia) Sdn Bhd, Times Subang, Lot 46, Subang Hi-Tech Industrial Park, Batu Tiga, 40000 Shah Alam, Selangor Darul Ehsan, Malaysia

Marshall Cavendish is a trademark of Times Publishing Limited

All websites were available and accurate when this book was sent to press.

Library of Congress Cataloging-in-Publication Data

Grayson, Robert.
  Military / Robert Grayson.
    p. cm. – (Working animals)
  Includes index.
  Summary: "Describes animals, including elephants, dogs, horses, mules, sea lions, dolphins, rats, and homing pigeons, which provide valuable service to the military"–Provided by publisher.
  ISBN 978-1-60870-164-3
  1. Animals–War use–Juvenile literature. I. Title.
  UH87.G73 2010
  355.4'24-dc22
                                    2010007007

Editorial and design by
Amber Books Ltd
Bradley's Close
74–77 White Lion Street
London N1 9PF
United Kingdom
www.amberbooks.co.uk

Project Editor: James Bennett
Copy Editor: Peter Mavrikis
Design: Andrew Easton
Picture Research: Terry Forshaw, Natascha Spargo

Printed in China
135642

CONTENTS

Chapter 1
Call to Service

Often lost in the history of military conflicts are the contributions made by animals on the battlefield. Dating back to the earliest days of warfare, animals have served bravely, but their efforts have usually been overlooked or unnoticed.

Elephants on the Battlefield

Elephants were used as a fighting force as far back as three thousand years ago. In ancient times, these massive animals, weighing as much as 11,000 pounds (5,000 kilograms) and standing as tall as 7½ feet (2.3 meters), were used like bulldozers or tanks to tear down enemy defenses, scatter the opposition's forces, and break through its ranks. There was not much an army without elephants could do to stop these hard-charging and intelligent animals.

◀ A military dog and his U.S Marine handler patrol an island in the Pacific during World War II.

▲ Hannibal, a North African general, used elephants to attack the army of ancient Rome.

"At times, advancing armies would tie swords to the ends of their elephants' tusks to make them appear even more ferocious."

Even fortresses could not keep these giants of the battlefield from destroying defensive walls and muscling through gates. At times, advancing armies would tie swords to the ends of their elephants' tusks to make them appear even more ferocious. The famous Greek conqueror Alexander the Great (356 BCE–323 BCE) was known to have used elephants in battle. The enormous creatures opposed his armies as well, especially in battles that took place in India.

▼ **Even in modern times, elephants have been used in the military. Here a team transports heavy artillery and equipment in India in the 1930s.**

About a hundred years after Alexander, the North African military commander Hannibal of Carthage became famous for his use of elephants. He gave them a major role in the Second Punic War (218 BCE–201 BCE) against Rome. Hannibal marched his men and elephants across the Iberian Peninsula, over the Pyrenees and then the Alps, finally entering northern Italy. Carthaginian soldiers also built special rafts to carry war elephants across the Rhone River in France to engage enemy troops stationed on the other side. Some of the elephants went into

Elephant Brigade

During World War II, the British army used elephants in Burma to build bridges and to help transport heavy materials through the jungle. In March 1944 the opposing Japanese army launched a major attack against the British strongholds in Burma. In response, the British decided to move the elephants up a steep mountain—some 5,000 feet (1,524 meters) high—to an area where they felt the Japanese couldn't find the beasts. They feared that otherwise the hardworking elephants might be captured or killed by the attacking enemy.

Leading the way up the mountain was a forty-six-year-old male elephant named Bandoola. The other elephants looked up to him as their leader. Bandoola managed to get his fellow elephants to follow him through seemingly impassable mountain trails, walking cautiously along 3-foot (1-meter) wide paths so as not to loosen the earth and plunge down the mountainside to their deaths. Like the best mountain climbers, the lead elephant had a strong sense about where he could walk safely, and he knew not to look down during the dangerous trip.

Bandoola's only misstep came when he reached the mountaintop and celebrated by breaking into a pineapple grove and eating nine hundred pineapples. He eventually recovered from the stomachache that followed.

"During World Wars I and II, elephants pulled heavy equipment into areas where motorized vehicles could not go. At times elephants were joined in this effort by oxen."

The Ultimate Sacrifice

During the Civil War (1861–1865), horses were so highly valued that they were considered important targets on the battlefield. It is estimated that more than 1.5 million horses were killed during the war, with over 3,000 horses killed during the bloody Battle of Gettysburg alone. The average life expectancy of a military horse in the Civil War was six months, as both sides were committed to battling on horseback. Most of the horses were well trained for battle and would not retreat, despite the often noisy and chaotic battlefield conditions. Forging ahead through fierce combat in the muddy battlefield terrain, refusing to retreat no matter how blinding and choking the dust, these horses did everything their riders demanded of them and often fought to their death.

battle without riders to charge opponents, inflict damage, and crush the enemy. Other elephants battled as mounts, with each one carrying on its back one or two soldiers or a carriage that could hold up to four warriors, each battling foes from different directions and from a position of height.

Elephants have played a part in modern warfare as well. During World Wars I and II, elephants pulled heavy equipment into areas where motorized vehicles could not go. At times elephants were joined in this effort by oxen. Oxen had been used in wars in the past, but usually only as **draft animals**.

Camels in Desert Warfare

Camels also have been used in battle for thousands of years, mostly in the

▶ **In India during World War II, an elephant easily lifts a fuel drum onto a plane.**

> **"Most horses do not like the smell of camels. When a horse and rider get close to a camel, the horse will usually refuse to go forward."**

Middle East and North Africa. Camels are at their best in the hot desert, where their footing is steady on the shifting sands. Camels can travel great distances without food and water. In fact, a rider usually gets tired well before his camel does.

Camels have another valuable trait: they stay calm under attack and do not panic at the sound of gunfire.

Most horses do not like the smell of camels. When a horse and rider get close to a camel, the horse will usually refuse to go forward. This

▲ **Moroccan soldiers patrol the western Sahara with their camels in 1980, following a dispute over the territory's independence.**

makes an attacking soldier on horseback **vulnerable** to a fighter riding a camel.

Because camels have few natural enemies, they rarely have a need to run. As a result, camels tend to be slower than horses, so they're not the animal of choice when a soldier needs to make a quick getaway. Camels are still used in the Middle East, especially by **guerrilla** forces that lack modern-day equipment.

Soldiers on Horseback

For more than five thousand years, horses have played an important role in military actions all over the world. Throughout history, nothing has been valued on the battlefield as much as a good horse. In medieval times knights in heavy armor would ride into battle on big heavy horses that were also protected by armor. Sometimes the armor on both the knight and the horse was so heavy

▲ **Horses were highly valued during the Civil War. Unfortunately, many of them were killed in battle.**

" ... on the Western Front in World War I (1914–1918), many battles were fought on horseback, though horses were starting to be eased out in favor of tanks. "

that the animal sank into the mud on soaking-wet battlefields.

Presidents George Washington, Andrew Jackson, Ulysses S. Grant, and Theodore Roosevelt were all outstanding horsemen. Horses were used to fight in all wars in the United States, including the American Revolution and the Civil War, and they were vital to settling the West. The U.S. **Cavalry** employed millions of horses throughout its long history.

In early combat on the Western Front in World War I (1914–1918), many battles were fought on horseback, though horses were starting to be eased out in favor of tanks. On the Eastern Front, the British Cavalry, well trained in mounted warfare, played a major role in the fighting. Horses, mules, and donkeys were also brought in as pack animals throughout the war.

During World War II (1939–1945), mounted warriors were key players in many nations' armies, including the Polish military in 1939, as it tried to fight off the German invaders. Both the German and the Russian armies used horses throughout the war. British troops fought a number of battles on horseback, with the last cavalry attack taking place in March 1942 against Japanese forces in Burma. U.S. mounted troops launched charges against the Japanese during the invasion of the Philippines and even managed to hold off tank attacks while on horseback. Once again, horses, mules, and donkeys were used as pack animals by nations in that war.

▶ **British soldiers on horseback make a charge through a smoke-covered battlefield in North Africa during World War II.**

▲ **Polish cavalrymen and their mounts during World War II.**

Pigeon Post

Pigeons have often been the unsung heroes of the battlefield. Messenger pigeons were used as early as 1150 BCE to send urgent news from the battlefield to military headquarters. At the end of the famous Battle of Waterloo, fought in Belgium in 1815, the First Duke of Wellington sent word to England that he had defeated the French Emperor Napoleon Bonaparte. Both human and pigeon messengers were assigned to deliver the good news. The pigeon arrived days before the human courier.

During the two world wars, pigeons delivered messages. One French homing pigeon by the name of Cher Ami was awarded the nation's Croix de Guerre (Cross of War) medal for service in World War I. The brave bird delivered twelve vital messages, including one sent after the winged courier was severely wounded. In World War II, thirty-two pigeons were given medals for saving human lives.

A Gentle Giant

During World War II, a Syrian brown bear cub, whose mother had just died, was found by soldiers from the 22nd Artillery Supply Corps of the Polish army as they made their way through northern Iran toward Palestine. Named Voytek ("smiling warrior" in Polish), he became attached to one of the soldiers, Lance Corporal Peter Prendys, who used some old bottles to feed the young bear condensed milk.

The bear picked up many human traits, like walking on two feet. A gentle giant, Voytek would ride with Prendys in the passenger seat of his military truck. After watching the soldiers unload ammunition from the truck several times, Voytek soon began helping with the unloading. The bear grew to 500 pounds (227 kilograms). Despite his size, he stayed with the unit throughout the war.

One day Voytek wandered into the shower hut in the unit's camp and happened on a spy who had climbed in through a window. The spy was drawing a map of the Polish camp so that enemy troops could steal the ammunition being stored there. The surprised spy let out a yell when the bear appeared and Polish troops came running in to investigate the commotion. The spy was captured and confessed to the plot. Voytek's shower antics made him an international hero.

▲ **Voytek the Soldier Bear, shown during his retirement at the Edinburgh Zoo in Scotland, where he spent his days after serving with the Polish military.**

Chapter 2
Canines on the Front Lines

For thousands of years, dogs have served bravely in battle, often on the front lines. Even in today's military conflicts, canines continue to fight against the enemy side by side with their human counterparts.

In ancient Rome, the military brought Molossus dogs into battle. It is believed that the ancient Greeks used these dogs as well. The Molossus, now extinct, was a strong and powerful breed. The dogs were usually sent by the Romans into battle wearing a spiked metal collar. Sometimes the Romans had these attack dogs lead their soldiers into battle. The Molossus is thought to be an ancestor of such modern breeds as the Mastiff, the Saint Bernard, and the Greater Swiss Mountain Dog.

French Emperor Napoleon Bonaparte enlisted a number of

◀ **A modern-day canine serves on the battlefields of Afghanistan.**

▲ **This statue of a Molossus dog is on display at the British Museum in London.**

Lost, Found, and Returned

Some of the world's greatest military leaders took their pets with them when they went off to war. U.S. General George Patton, for instance, was accompanied everywhere by his white bull terrier, Willie. U.S. Army Brigadier General Alexander S. Asboth's setter, named York, went into battle with him during the Civil War.

During the American Revolution, George Washington brought his American staghound, Sweet Lips, with him to the front. Apparently, British General William Howe brought his pet dog as well. While surveying the battlefield after the Battle of Germantown in October 1777, Washington saw a small dog wandering around. A dog lover, Washington went to the aid of the pooch. Much to his surprise, the dog had a collar, showing that the friendly canine belonged to General Howe.

Realizing how upset Howe must have been without his faithful animal companion, Washington arranged for a temporary truce with the British so the dog could be returned to Howe. Along with the dog, the American general sent a note to Howe, telling him it was with pleasure that he was returning the dog that had accidentally fallen into American hands. General Howe called the dog's return an "honorable act," one that earned Washington great respect from his British adversary.

▲ **George Washington is one of many great leaders to have valued the companionship of his pet dog.**

"In World War I, dogs delivered weapons, helped the wounded, and served as messengers, sentries, scouts, and trackers."

fighting dogs in his army as he attempted to conquer Europe in the early 1800s. As time went by, dogs took on other roles in the military besides that of attacker. In World War I, dogs delivered weapons, helped the wounded, and served as messengers, sentries, scouts, and trackers. Many nations on both sides of the conflict employed dogs in their military ranks. Dogs of all breeds served and were assigned jobs they were best suited for, based on their size, speed, intelligence, and age.

Missions of Mercy

France and England trained dogs to search World War I battlefields for wounded soldiers. The dogs carried packs with medical supplies, water, and food for the wounded to use

until help arrived. Once the dogs found a soldier in need, they returned to camp and led medical personnel back to the fallen warrior.

Sometimes two-wheeled carts, pulled by large dogs, transported badly injured soldiers from the front

▶ **There are many memorials to dogs who have served in war, including this one in New Hampshire.**

"The dogs that helped the wounded got the name 'mercy dogs,' for the work they did. Several thousand mercy dogs served in World War I."

lines to aid stations. Dogs offered two key advantages over horses when it came to doing this job: they presented a smaller target for the enemy, and they could work alone, while horses needed soldiers to lead them.

The dogs that helped the wounded got the name "mercy dogs," for the work they did. Several thousand mercy dogs served in World War I. Countless soldiers owed their lives to the dedication and kindness of these dogs. During one battle, for example, a French dog named Prusco located and saved more than one hundred soldiers. An amazing feat! When the large, wolflike dog spotted wounded soldiers, it would drag them into protective holes before returning to the aid station to get human assistance.

Carrying Messages

Messenger dogs in World War I were fast and well trained. They had to make it through **trenches**, barbed wire, and chemical gas. These dogs carried out their assignments wearing specially designed gas masks. One

▲ **Both German soldiers and their dogs wore gas masks in the trenches during World War I.**

▶ **A U.S. Marine and his loyal canine companion train for warfare at Camp Lejeune, North Carolina, in 1943.**

" The dog ... delivered the message to the Belgian command post in time for reinforcements to be sent to save the battered Belgian fighters. "

Belgian battalion, under assault from the Germans, was in desperate need of reinforcements. The Germans had cut the communication lines of the Belgian fighters. The Belgians' only hope was a trained dog that was on the front lines with them.

The dog was sent to deliver a message to the Belgian headquarters. He moved quickly, dodging heavy artillery fire, and delivered the message to the Belgian command post in time for reinforcements to be sent to save the battered Belgian fighters.

▲ **U.S. Marines on Bougainville Island in the Pacific, with highly trained dogs by their side, track down Japanese snipers in the swamps during World War II.**

Smallest Hero

One of the smallest heroes of all time is Smoky, a brave Yorkshire terrier who stood just 7 inches (18 centimeters) tall and weighed a mere 4 pounds (1.8 kilograms). Found in a foxhole by American soldiers in a New Guinea jungle in February 1944 during World War II, the dog was adopted by Corporal William A. Wynne. Wynne used to carry Smoky in his backpack, and she survived eighteen months of combat with him. During downtime Wynne taught Smoky many tricks. One of those tricks made her a hero.

The military needed to get a telegraph wire under a crucial airfield in the Philippines. Tunneling would have taken three days, but Wynne realized that Smoky could carry the wire in no time through a 70-foot (21-meter) pipe that ran under the field. The one hitch was that the pipe was just 8 inches (20 centimeters) in diameter and soil sifted into the pipe at some places, leaving only about 4 inches (10 centimeters) of headroom for Smoky. But just as Wynne had taught her, the dog carried the wire through the pipe and the mission was a success.

Smoky also worked as a therapy dog at an American military hospital in New Guinea. After the war, she was taken to the United States, where she continued her hospital work, bringing cheerful comfort to many patients.

▲ **Smoky prepares to carry the telegraph wire through the pipe under the airfield.**

> ***Chips...battled with the enemy inside the bunker, forcing the soldiers to run outside, where they were then captured by the Americans. It was just one of many times that Chips acted heroically during eight brutal battles.*"**

Every major country that fought in World War I had a program to train military dogs. Only the United States did not, and it relied instead on dogs taught by the French and the British. By World War II, however, the United States had a fully trained canine (K-9) force. During that conflict, thousands of dogs once again served valiantly in armies all over the world.

Outfoxing the Enemy

Chips was considered one of the bravest members of the U.S. K-9 Corps. He was a mixed-breed dog—though mostly German shepherd. Chips was assigned to General George Patton's Seventh Army and traveled all over Europe throughout World War II. In 1943, while on a beach during the invasion of Sicily, Chips's unit came under heavy fire. Enemy troops were concealed in a bunker and shooting at will. They had the whole American unit pinned down. Chips broke free of his handler and raced into the bunker, carefully avoiding gunfire all along the way.

Once there, he battled with the enemy inside the bunker, forcing the soldiers to run outside, where they were then captured by the Americans. It was just one of many times that Chips acted heroically during eight brutal battles. He was awarded a Silver Star for his extraordinary efforts and a Purple Heart for injuries he received during battle.

Those medals were later taken away because dogs were considered "equipment" in the U.S. military, and that made them ineligible to receive medals. To members of his unit, however, the brave canine didn't need medals. Chips had earned the respect of every soldier who ever fought alongside him. In 1990 Disney made a movie, *Chips, the War Dog*, about his life on the front lines.

Sniffing Out Bombs

Following World War II, dogs continued to prove their worth on the battlefield. In the Vietnam War, more than four thousand dogs served with the U.S. military between 1961 and 1975. A majority of them died during the fighting. Dogs were on the front lines in the Persian Gulf War (1990–1991), and they continue to

▲ **Chips, one of the most famous and gallant U.S. war dogs ever, is shown during the Sicilian Campaign in 1944, angling for a doughnut from a GI.**

Lifesavers

Military dogs played an important role in the Vietnam War and are credited with saving at least ten thousand lives during the conflict. Fighting in the jungles of Vietnam was very difficult for American soldiers, who were unused to the terrain and climate. The thick plant growth also limited what they could see and hear. It was tough by day, worse at night. A canine's superior senses of hearing and smell were able to tip off soldiers to countless unforeseen dangers. The dogs were especially good at detecting mines, trip wires, and booby traps. The dogs could sense enemy troops lying in ambush or pick up a sniper sitting in a tree or hiding in the forest. The dogs also worked to detect underground tunnels that enemy forces used to sneak into American-controlled territory. They helped with night scouting and with guarding strategic airfields.

The dogs underwent intensive twelve-week training programs that focused on jungle combat. The canines were taught to respond to both voice commands and hand signals. The dogs were so effective, the enemy offered a reward for anyone who killed a U.S. military dog and its handler.

▲ **A U.S. Marine helps defend a South Vietnamese village during the Vietnam War by patrolling areas around the village with the help of his German shepherd.**

serve in many capacities in Iraq and Afghanistan with U.S. troops today.

One of the K-9 Corps' most vital roles is to sniff out bombs, and they regularly save hundreds of lives by detecting these devices before they go off. Specially trained military dogs and their handlers patrol airports, train stations, bus terminals, and government buildings in major cities throughout the world to help detect any possible terrorist activities.

▲ **A U.S. Air Force officer and his dog, Rocco, search for explosives near Balad Air Base in Iraq.**

Chapter 3
Clearing Mines, Detecting Explosives

For decades, land mines have been used in warfare all around the world. The mines are responsible for maiming or killing hundreds of thousands of soldiers and civilians, and they continue to threaten the lives of many people today.

Mines are easy and cheap to build, and almost every fighting force has access to the instructions and materials needed to make the deadly devices. Once the conflicts are over, nobody bothers to remove the unexploded bombs from the ground. They remain in place, waiting for some unsuspecting civilian—usually a child—to accidentally set them off.

The United Nations estimates that civilian injuries from undetected land mines average as high as twenty thousand a year. The mines can be found in some fifty-eight countries,

◄ **A U.S. Navy patrol dog inspects a vehicle for explosives in Kuwait in 2003.**

▲ **This dog is being trained to detect land mines in Bosnia.**

Dogged Determination

Dogs that sniff out explosives are never off duty, and no dog proved that better than Carlo, a large Belgian Malinois, or shepherd dog. The Belgian Malinois has a brownish yellow coat and a black muzzle, cheeks, and ears, resembling a German shepherd. The breed is good at detection, search-and-rescue, and explosives work. During the Persian Gulf War in 1991, Carlo detected 167 hideouts of explosives, many of which were set to go off if someone simply touched them.

Carlo's handler, U.S. Air Force Staff Sergeant Christopher Batta, was with his dog for every one of the brave canine's finds. For instance, the dog courageously refused to back down while stubbornly barking at a stack of cases of MREs (Meals Ready-to-Eat). A careful examination of the cases proved that the meals were booby-trapped with a cluster of explosives set to go off on contact. Hundreds of lives were saved as a result of Carlo's unwavering determination to have the cases of meals checked.

Sergeant Batta was awarded a Bronze Star in October 1991 for his service in Kuwait, with Carlo standing by his side.

▲ **Explosives detection work continues in Iraq and other dangerous places. Here U.S. Air Force Staff Sergeant Joseph Branch searches cars with his dog, Nemo, at a checkpoint in Baghdad.**

❝Dogs have proved to be indispensable when it comes to the extremely dangerous task of mine removal.❞

including Bosnia, Sri Lanka, Tanzania, and Mozambique.

Canine Lifesavers

The job of finding these lethal land mines, either during wartime or after a conflict is over, primarily falls to specially trained K-9 units. Dogs have proved to be indispensable when it comes to the extremely dangerous task of mine removal.

Dogs are trained in obedience before taking on fourteen weeks of mine-clearing exercises in their home countries. Then the dogs and their handlers go to the country where

▲ **This U.S. Army K-9 team is carrying out the dangerous assignment of detecting unexploded land mines at Bagram Air Field, Afghanistan.**

“Not long ago, the dogs were joined by a new group of fearless land-mine detectives: rats.”

they will work and undergo another ten weeks of training before they actually start to search for live mines.

Dogs are taught to sniff for the mines. A dog's sense of smell is one thousand times sharper than that of a human being. The canines do a much better job at detecting the bombs than metal detectors do because not all land mines are wrapped in metal casings. Many land mines are enclosed in plastic cases. Dogs can detect the odor of plastic as well as TNT and other explosives. They can also learn to sniff out metallic wire. Dogs can smell a land mine that is buried up to 4 inches (10 centimeters) underground.

Both female and male dogs are trained to detect mines. A dog usually works with the same handler throughout its career, and the two must forge a strong bond to work together successfully. Even dogs that sniff out mines regularly continue a daily training program to make sure they do not forget any of their lessons. If dogs start their training in mine clearing at about a year old, they can continue to work for about six years before retiring.

Rat Patrol

German shepherds, Belgian Malinois, Labrador retrievers, and golden retrievers work all over the world in mine detection. Not long ago, the dogs were joined by a new group of fearless land-mine detectives: rats. Nobody has ever liked to see rats in their neighborhood, but now these small creatures are proving their worth when it comes to ridding the world of mines.

▶ **A specially trained rat sniffs out land mines in Mozambique, Africa.**

"*Specially trained marine mammals help the U.S. Navy locate unexploded mines in places like the Persian Gulf.*"

The special mine-clearing talents of rats were discovered during an experiment in Africa several years ago. Realizing that rats have an acute sense of smell, researchers from Belgium and Tanzania decided to try to train them to sniff for vapors coming from the explosives packed underground. The rats were taught what to sniff for within a controlled area and then tested. If they found the mine, the researchers trained the rats to scratch the surface near where the device was located. If they followed through, they were rewarded with food. The rats were trained over and over again, and the program became a success.

The rats require a handler and need to be kept on a long rope or a leash. Although the rats work well with humans, the rodents do not have to form a bond with just one person and can team up with a different handler every day, which is a plus. There's another plus in using rats: if the lightweight rodents accidentally step on one of the deadly mines, the mine will not explode. Another advantage of sending in rats is that they are easy to handle and inexpensive to transport. A whole team of rats can be shipped to a mine-infested area on very little notice. The rats have been doing an excellent job of mine clearing in Africa.

Underwater Operatives

When it comes to finding mines in the water, the U.S. Navy has some very unusual secret weapons: dolphins and sea lions. The specially trained marine mammals help the navy locate unexploded mines in places like the Persian Gulf.

▶ **A U.S. Navy dolphin named K-Dog leaps from the water during training.**

❝These mammals are taught not to touch a mine. They simply locate the devices and, through a camera attached to their bodies, transmit pictures back to their handlers.❞

It is believed that dolphins have been trained for mine clearing since the mid-1960s. Sea lions were not recruited until much later. The dolphins are used for their superior sense of hearing. These mammals are taught not to touch a mine. They simply locate the devices and, through a camera attached to their bodies, transmit pictures back to their handlers. Once navy divers know where the mines are, they can go into the water and safely defuse them. Sea lions also have excellent hearing and eyesight and, like dolphins, they are very intelligent.

▲ A bottlenose dolphin communicates with its trainer in the waters off Hawaii.

▶ Well-trained and alert, this sea lion is clearly a valuable asset to the navy.

Chapter 4
The Specialists

Some animals have special skills. Combining their keen senses, strength, and stamina, these "specialists" can accomplish missions that even modern technology cannot match.

Running Silent, Running Deep

Sea lions are not only great at clearing mines. They are strong, clever creatures that can be trained to spot unwelcome intruders in both open waters and harbors with obstacles like docks and piers. The U.S. Navy has taught sea lions to detect swimmers near sensitive places like naval bases, where submarines and other top-secret equipment are kept.

Sea lions are very quiet swimmers, and they can dive into deep waters, making it hard for human swimmers

◄ **A sea lion and his trainer at the Space and Naval Warfare Systems Center in San Diego, California**

▲ **Sea lions can swim faster and quieter underwater than any human diver.**

Ceremonial Duties

Fighting units throughout the world no longer use as many horses as they once did, but that doesn't mean the four-legged warriors no longer have a military presence. In India, the army's 61st Cavalry remains active as a fighting force, and China has several battalions of horse soldiers patrolling border areas. Many nations continue to train their horses for battle but use them mostly just for ceremonies. Cavalry units appear in parades, military funerals, and government events in such diverse countries as the United States, France, Italy, the United Kingdom, Russia, Poland, Canada, Chile, Brazil, Spain, Denmark, and Portugal.

▲ **India's 61st Cavalry is unusual in that it remains an active fighting force.**

“Sea lions, as well as some dolphins, are also trained to swim alongside ships to spot terrorists who might try to attach an explosive device to the vessels.”

to detect them. In their mouths, each sea lion carries a clamp, which is attached to a long restraining rope. When an intruder is spotted, the sea lion swiftly attaches the clamp to the suspect's leg. Then the highly trained mammal pushes an alarm button attached to a pier or ship to let the navy divers know an intruder has been captured.

Sea lions, as well as some dolphins, are also trained to swim alongside ships to spot terrorists who might try to attach an explosive device to the vessels. Again, an alarm button is attached to the

▲ **Underwater, the sea lion carries a clamp that it can use to capture unwanted visitors.**

"Water buffalo are experts when it comes to getting through the rough terrain of Brazil's Amazon region."

outside of the ship so the sea mammals can alert the crew.

Water Buffalo on Patrol

Water buffalo are experts when it comes to getting through the rough terrain of Brazil's Amazon region. That is why the Brazilian Army has drafted them into service. The 1,100-pound (500- kilogram) animals carry equipment along Brazil's treacherous 6,800-mile (11,200- kilometer) border and help soldiers patrol the area. The territory is made up of narrow trails and thick jungle. The army must have a presence there because drug dealers and diamond smugglers often use the Amazon as a hideout.

Motor vehicles are useless in the Amazon because the army cannot get fuel to the area. The water buffalo are fueled by the plants they eat in the jungle. They are also well adapted to the rain forest and are better at warding off the diseases that other pack animals are vulnerable to.

Mules and Donkeys: Mountain Climbers Extraordinaire

Even in this high-tech age, the United States has to rely on an old-fashioned mode of transportation to get supplies and equipment to troops in the mountainous regions of Afghanistan. The terrain is so difficult to navigate that even helicopters and Humvee vehicles are of little use there. Mules and donkeys handle this critical mission. For them to do their jobs, however, the U.S. military must train soldiers to pack these animals properly.

This training takes place at the U.S. Marine Corps Mountain Warfare

▶ **In Afghanistan, mules are crucial to the military.**

« Packing mules properly helps members of the military get to their destinations faster, and that may mean saving lives. »

Training Center in California. In 1914 the U.S. Army issued a manual on how to pack animals in wartime. Not much has changed since then, but most soldiers have no experience in working with pack animals until they reach the training center.

Besides learning how to pack mules, the soldiers gain an understanding of mules and donkeys. Trainees are amazed to learn that these animals know three steps ahead where they want to walk along a sharp, rocky trail. Soldiers report working with the

◀ **Mules try to move an American ammunition wagon along a muddy road in France during World War I.**

▲ **Soldiers take to the water to lead mules across a river in Burma (Myanmar) during World War II.**

Hero Horsemen

Even in modern warfare, it never hurts to know how to ride a horse. Responding quickly to the September 11, 2001, terrorist attacks, the United States sent a team of highly trained special forces to Afghanistan on a top-secret mission. Their goal was to attack the Taliban stronghold city of Mazar-i-Sharif. The Americans, aided by their Afghan allies, would have to pass through heavily armed Taliban and al-Qaeda territory. They would also have to go over treacherous mountains to get to their goal. There was only one way to cross those mountains, and that was on horseback. The Americans and their allies succeeded in their mission. They captured hundreds of Taliban fighters, all because of a secret weapon: the horse.

▲ **U.S. Special Forces gallop through a riverbed in northern Afghanistan to pursue al-Qaeda and Taliban fugitives believed to be operating in the area.**

same mules for years and never seeing them stumble. Packing mules properly helps members of the military get to their destinations faster, and that may mean saving lives. These animals also carry the sick and wounded out of the mountains to aid stations where they can be treated.

Sheep and Goats: Fighting Fires

Since 1999, sheep and goats have been working with the Utah National Guard to help stop deadly wildfires near its training facility. The fires usually start because of the enormous amounts of oak brush and sagebrush that grow in the fields around Camp Williams near Salt Lake City. The fires require long, difficult hours to battle and present a danger to property and life.

The sheep and goats eat the dry brush right down to the stubble, so if a fire does break out, there is little to fuel it and the blaze can be put out quickly. More than 1,200 sheep and goats serve as munching heroes.

Chapter 5
Career Guide

If you like the idea of working with animals as a career, the military offers many opportunities. Animals in the armed services need veterinarians as well as veterinary technicians, animal-behavior specialists, trainers, and handlers.

The United States has a large veterinary service unit called the Veterinary Corps. It takes care of all military animals in the U.S. Army, Air Force, Marines, and Navy. More than 700 veterinarians, as well as 1,800 soldiers, work for the Veterinary Corps. In addition, 400 civilians work for the unit, and that number continues to grow.

Dogs that serve with the U.S. military in various capacities get a physical exam every six months. The navy's Marine Mammal Program has a veterinarian and a veterinary technician on call twenty-four hours a day, seven days a week. The program also employs biologists.

◄ **A U.S. Air Force officer and his dog search a car in Germany.**

▲ **Military dog Valerie is given hand commands by a U.S. Navy dog trainer.**

Research Positions

Researchers in the military work on ways to keep animals healthy and safe. For instance, dogs were recently outfitted with new vests to help them avoid getting wounded on the battlefield. The old vests protected them from stab wounds, while the new vests are both stabproof and bulletproof. The vests cover a dog's upper body from the shoulders to the stomach area.

Veterinary specialists study the effects of combat on animals such as dogs. War can have an emotional effect on canines as well as humans. Animal-behavior specialists in the military help keep the canines healthy by identifying an emotional problem and helping the animal overcome it.

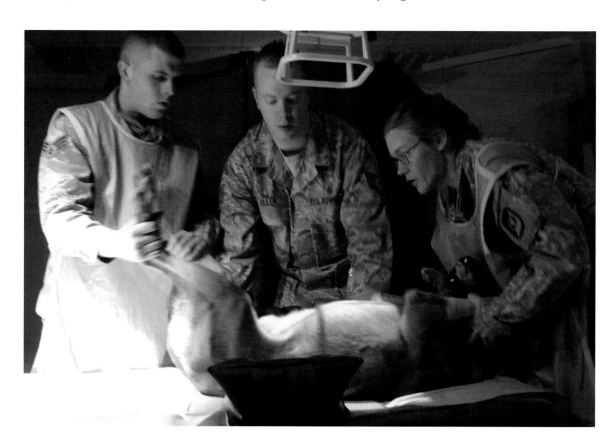

◄ **Both soldier and dog are well protected as they patrol a checkpoint in Fallujah, Iraq.**

▲ **Canine health is of prime importance in the military. Here a dog undergoes an X-ray by a veterinary team.**

" A handler must be someone in the security forces field, and it helps if he or she had some previous experience working with animals before entering the military. "

Dog Handlers

Many people who serve in the military ask to partner with the brave dogs that sniff out bombs, search for weapons, or stand guard against terrorists. Not everyone can qualify for a military career as a dog handler.

Getting into the program is not easy, and training to work with the dogs is intense. A handler must be someone in the security forces field of the military, and it helps if he or she had some previous experience working with animals before entering the

▲ **In Australia, a handler and his dog guard a B-2 stealth bomber.**

A Special Bond

Dog handlers in the U.S. military get very close to their four-legged partners. These brave canines save many lives; some have even saved their own handlers' lives. So when it comes time for a military dog to retire, it is easy to understand why its handler often wants to be the one to give it a permanent home. Today, once a dog is retired and cleared for adoption by the military, the dog's handler is generally the first to be offered the opportunity to adopt the animal.

Handlers realize the stress the dogs endured while serving in the military, and they want to make sure the canines live out their lives comfortably. One of the biggest concerns is health care. Because of a dog's active military life, it often develops costly physical ailments later in life. The handler is usually most willing to care for the dog and get it the medical care it needs.

▲ **Years facing dangerous missions together, a dog and his handler form bonds that last a lifetime.**

▲ Meky, a military dog, sits beside his handler, ready for his next dangerous assignment.

military. Before being accepted as a handler trainee, a person must spend at least fourteen hours accompanying a handler to get a feel for what the job is like.

People chosen to become animal handlers must attend a three-and-a-half-month training program at the Lackland Air Force Base in San Antonio, Texas. Often, new handlers train with experienced dogs for a while and newly recruited dogs train with experienced handlers before the new handlers and new dogs are teamed up. Training is constant for the pair once a handler and dog are put together. They are recertified for their jobs every year.

A dog and handler can get an assignment in a war zone, on a military base, or guarding a building and looking for explosives at a civilian site. Today military forces in many countries use dogs and handlers to guard airports, bus terminals, and other sites that may be considered targets of terrorists.

Stubby

Stubby, a stray pit bull, was found during the summer of 1917 in Hartford, Connecticut, near the training camp of the 102nd Infantry. Robert Conroy, a member of the 102nd, took him in and the dog became the military unit's mascot. When the 102nd left for France in World War I, Stubby was not supposed to go, but Convoy smuggled him aboard his ship. Although he had no formal training, the small dog knew what was expected of him. While on the battlefield with the 102nd, Stubby often guarded the men while they slept. One night he bit an enemy soldier who was trying to infiltrate the American camp. Another time Stubby smelled gas and awakened the soldiers, giving them time to put on their gas masks. The dog spent nineteen months overseas, participating in many battles.

Glossary

cavalry
a military unit that fights on horseback

counterparts
persons, objects, or animals that are very much like or equal to one another

draft animals
animals used for pulling loads

guerrillas
small bands of soldiers who are not part of the regular army of a country; guerrillas usually fight the enemy by making quick, surprise attacks

trenches
long, narrow ditches

vulnerable
at risk, open to attack

Further Information

BOOKS

Cooper, Jilly. *Animals in War: Valiant Horses, Courageous Dogs, and Other Unsung Animal Heroes.* Guilford, CT: Globe Pequot Press, 2002.

Greenwood, Mark. *The Donkey of Gallipoli: A True Story of Courage in World War I.* Cambridge, MA: Candlewick Press, 2008.

Hamer, Blythe. *Dogs at War: True Stories of Canine Courage under Fire.* London: Carlton Books, 2001.

Kadohata, Cynthia. *Cracker! The Best Dog in Vietnam.* New York: Atheneum Books, 2007.

Lemish, Michael. *War Dogs: A History of Loyalty and Heroism.* Washington, D.C.: Brassey's, Inc., 1996.

WEBSITES

http://community-2.webtv.net/Hahn-50thAP-K9/K9History/
This comprehensive site focuses on dogs that have served in the military in the United States and the United Kingdom.

http://www.war-dogs.com/
A site dedicated to war dogs and their handlers.

http://animalsinwar.org.uk/
The official site of the Animals in War Memorial Fund.

http://www.pigeoncenter.org/militarypigeons.html
The World of Wings Center's website focuses on the life-saving actions of birds that served in the military during wartime.

http://www.militaryworkingdogs.com
The official site of the Military Working Dog Foundation.

Index

PICTURE CREDITS

The photographs in this book are used by permission and through the courtesy of:

Alamy: 21 (Erin Paul Donovan)

Cody Images: 11

Corbis: 6 (Bettmann), 7 (Gianni Dagli Orti), 8 (Hulton), 12 (Pascal Manoukian), 15 (Hulton), 16 (Bettmann), 18 (Chad Hunt), 22 (Bettmann), 23 (Bettmann), 24 (Hulton), 27 (Bettmann), 45 (Ed Darack/Science Faction), 49 (Ed Darack/Science Faction)

Fotolia: 2 (Steve Mann)

Getty Images: 28 (Rentmeester/Time Life), 35 (Alexander Joe/AFP), 42 (Christophe Archambault/AFP), 48 (Scott Nelson)

Library of Congress: 13

Photos.com: 20

Rex Features: 17 (Dave Crump), 52 (Sabah Ara)

U. S. Department of Defense: 29–33 (all), 37–41 (all), 43, 46, 47, 50, 51, 53–56

Wikipedia Creative Commons Licence: 19 (Mike Peel)

William A. Wynne © 2010 (smokywardog.com): 25 (from the book Yorkie Doodle Dandy)

ABOUT THE AUTHOR

Robert Grayson is an award-winning former daily newspaper reporter and magazine writer. He is the author of a number of books for young adults about both law enforcement and environmental activism. An animal lover, Robert has published numerous stories about animals that work on stage and screen. He has also contributed essays to the anthology *Pets Across America: Lessons Animals Teach Us*.